Native American Library

BLACKFOOT
History and Culture

Helen Dwyer and Mary Stout

Consultant Robert J. Conley
Sequoyah Distinguished Professor at Western Carolina University

Gareth Stevens
Publishing

Please visit our website, www.garethstevens.com. For a free color catalog of all our high-quality books, call toll free 1-800-542-2595 or fax 1-877-542-2596.

Library of Congress Cataloging-in-Publication Data

Stout, Mary, 1954-
Blackfoot history and culture / Mary Stout.
    p. cm. — (Native American library)
Includes index.
ISBN 978-1-4339-5956-1 (pbk.)
ISBN 978-1-4339-5957-8 (6-pack)
ISBN 978-1-4339-5954-7 (library binding)
1. Siksika Indians—Juvenile literature. I. Title.
E99.S54S76 2012
978.004'97352—dc22

                        2011002633

New edition published in 2012 by
Gareth Stevens Publishing
111 East 14th Street, Suite 349
New York, NY 10003

First edition published 2005 by Gareth Stevens Publishing

Copyright © 2012 Gareth Stevens Publishing

Produced by Discovery Books
Project editor: Helen Dwyer
Designer and page production: Sabine Beaupré
Photo researchers: Tom Humphrey and Helen Dwyer
Maps: Stefan Chabluk

Photo credits: Cover Paul Chesley/Getty Images; Corbis: pp. 14, 17, 19, 22, 31, 33, 34; Getty Images: pp. 29 (Buyenlarge), 38 (The Washington Post), 39 (The Washington Post); Gryffindor: p. 36; Karl Bodmer: p. 7; Mary Evans Picture Library: p. 16; Native Stock: pp. 10, 13, 18, 20, 21, 23, 24 (top), 25, 32, 35, 37 (top); Peter Newark's American Pictures: pp. 12, 15, 24 (bottom), 26, 27; Shutterstock: pp. 5, 28; Uyvsdi: p. 37 (bottom).

Printed in the United States of America

CPSIA compliance information: Batch #CS11GS: For further information contact Gareth Stevens, New York, New York at 1-800-542-2595.

CONTENTS

Words that appear in the glossary are printed in **boldface** type the first time they appear in the text.

INTRODUCTION

The Blackfoot are a people who inhabit the plains of Montana in the United States and the provinces of Saskatchewan and Alberta in Canada. They are just one of the many groups of Native Americans who live today in North America. There are well over five hundred Native American tribes in the United States and more than six hundred in Canada. At least three million people in North America consider themselves to be Native Americans. But who are Native Americans, and how do the Blackfoot fit into the history of North America's native peoples?

THE FIRST IMMIGRANTS

Native Americans are people whose **ancestors** settled in North America thousands of years ago. These ancestors probably came from eastern parts of Asia. Their **migrations** probably occurred during cold periods called **ice ages**. At these times, sea levels were much lower than they are now. The area between northeastern Asia and Alaska was dry land, so it was possible to walk between the continents.

Probable extent of dry land during the last ice age

CHUKCHI SEA

SIBERIA

Bering Strait

ALASKA

CANADA

BERING SEA   Anchorage

Siberia (Asia) and Alaska (North America) are today separated by an area of ocean named the Bering Strait. During the last ice age, the green area on this map was at times dry land. The Asian ancestors of the Blackfoot walked from one continent to the other.

The Cliff Palace at Mesa Verde, Colorado, is the most spectacular example of Native American culture that survives today. It consists of more than 150 rooms and pits built around A.D. 1200 from sandstone blocks.

Scientists are not sure when these migrations took place, but it must have been more than twelve thousand years ago. Around that time, water levels rose and covered the land between Asia and the Americas.

By around ten thousand years ago, the climate had warmed and was similar to conditions today. The first peoples in North America moved around the continent in small groups, hunting wild animals and collecting a wide variety of plant foods. Gradually these groups spread out and lost contact with each other. They developed separate cultures and adopted lifestyles that suited their **environments.**

SETTLING DOWN

Many tribes, including the ancestors of the Blackfoot, continued to live **nomadic** lives, gathering food and hunting or fishing. However, some Native Americans began to live in settlements and grow crops. Their homes ranged from underground pit houses and huts of mud and thatch to dwellings in cliffs. By 3500 B.C., a plentiful supply of fish in the Pacific Ocean and in rivers had enabled people to settle in large coastal villages from Alaska to Washington State. In the deserts of Arizona, more than two thousand years later, farmers constructed hundreds of miles of **irrigation** canals to carry water to their crops.

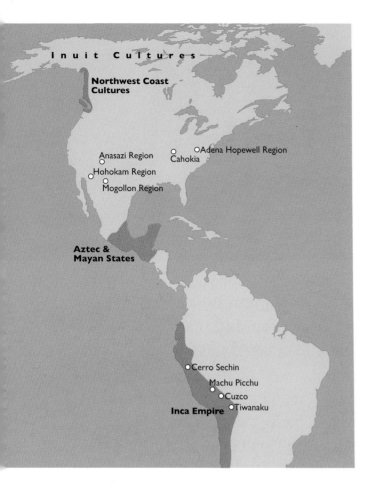

Inuit Cultures

Northwest Coast
Cultures

Anasazi Region

Hohokam Region

Mogollon Region

Cahokia

Adena Hopewell Region

Aztec &
Mayan States

Cerro Sechin

Machu Picchu

Cuzco

Inca Empire   Tiwanaku

This map highlights some of the main Native American cultures that flourished before the arrival of Europeans in the fifteenth century.

In the Ohio River valley between 700 B.C. and A.D. 500, people of the Adena and Hopewell **cultures** built clusters of large burial mounds, such as the Serpent Mound in Ohio, which survives today. In the Mississippi **floodplains**, the native peoples formed complex societies. They created mud and thatch temples on top of flat earth pyramids. Their largest town, Cahokia, in Illinois, contained more than one hundred mounds and may have been home to thirty thousand people.

The Blackfoot tribes are believed to have migrated about four hundred years ago to the Great Plains from the northeastern forests of present-day Maine and northeastern Canada. Their lifestyle changed to one based on hunting buffalo for food and clothing.

CONTACT WITH EUROPEANS

Around A.D. 1500, European ships reached North America. The first explorers were the Spanish. Armed with guns and riding horses, they took over land and forced the Native Americans to work for them. The Spanish were followed by the British, Dutch, and French, who were looking for land to settle and for opportunities to trade. The Blackfoot people first made contact with Europeans in 1690.

When Native Americans met these Europeans they came into contact with diseases, such as smallpox and measles, that they had never experienced before. At least one half of all Native Americans, and possibly many more than that, were unable to overcome these diseases and died.

Guns were also disastrous for Native Americans. At first, only the Europeans had guns, which enabled them to overcome native peoples in fights and battles. Eventually, Native American groups obtained guns and used them in conflicts with each other. Native American groups were also forced to take sides and fight in wars between the French and British.

Horses, too, had a big influence on Native American lifestyles, especially on the Great Plains. Some groups became horse breeders and traders. People were able to travel greater distances and began to hunt buffalo on horseback. Soon horses became central to Plains trade and social life.

In the middle of the eighteenth century, the Blackfoot obtained horses and guns from friendly tribes that traded with Europeans. However, the Blackfoot only began trading directly with Europeans in the 1780s.

At the end of the 1700s, people of European descent began to migrate over the Appalachian Mountains, looking for new land to farm and exploit. By the middle of the nineteenth century, they had reached the west coast of North America. This expansion was disastrous for Native Americans.

This illustration of a Blackfoot on horseback dates from the 1830s. Swiss artist Karl Bodmer traveled through the American West, painting pictures of the native peoples he met.

RESERVATION LIFE

Many peoples were pressured into moving onto **reservations** to the west. The biggest of these reservations later became the U.S. state of Oklahoma. Native Americans who tried to remain in their homelands were attacked and defeated.

The Blackfeet Reservation was established in Montana in 1873. This was followed a few years later by the creation of three separate Blackfoot reservations in Canada for the Piikani (Piegan), Siksika (Northern Blackfoot), and Kainai (Blood) tribes.

New laws in the United States and Canada took away most of the control Native Americans had over their lives. They were expected to give up their cultures and adopt the ways and habits of white Americans. It became a crime to practice their traditional religions. Children were taken from their homes and placed in **boarding schools**, where they were forbidden to speak their native languages.

Despite this **persecution**, many Native Americans clung on to their cultures through the first half of the twentieth century. The Society of American Indians was founded in 1911, and its campaign for U.S. citizenship for Native Americans was successful in 1924. Other Native American organizations were formed to promote traditional cultures and to campaign politically for Native American rights.

This map of North America highlights the main Native American cultural groups, along with the smaller groups, or tribes, featured in this series of books.

Blackfoot chief Mountain Chief (1848–1942) took part in a recording at the Smithsonian Institution in 1916. This was part of a project to record and investigate Native American history and culture.

THE ROAD TO SELF-GOVERNMENT

Despite these campaigns, Native Americans on reservations endured poverty and very low standards of living. Many of them moved away to work and live in cities, where they hoped life would be better. In most cases, they found life just as difficult. They not only faced **discrimination** and **prejudice** but also could not compete successfully for jobs against more established ethnic groups.

In the 1970s, the American Indian Movement (AIM) organized large protests that attracted attention worldwide. They highlighted the problems of unemployment, discrimination, and poverty that Native Americans experienced in North America.

The AIM protests led to changes in policy. Some new laws protected the civil rights of Native Americans, while other laws allowed tribal governments to be formed. Today tribal governments have a wide range of powers. They operate large businesses and run their own schools and health care.

LAND AND ORIGINS

Chapter 1

THE LAND OF THE BLACKFOOT

The Blackfoot are actually a **confederation** of separate tribes. The Kainai (also called Blood) with 9,400 members, the Siksika (or Northern Blackfoot) with 4,200 members, and the Piikani (or Piegan) with 2,800 members all live in Canada. With 15,560 members, the Southern Piegan call themselves Blackfeet and live in the United States. These tribes share the Algonquian language and have very similar cultures. In the past, the white newcomers to North America were confused about the tribes and thought them all the same. Today, the Blackfoot Confederacy is a political union of the different tribes that helps them all deal with the U.S. and Canadian governments.

IN THE BEGINNING

The Blackfoot people traditionally occupied an area east of the Rocky Mountains in Alberta, Saskatchewan, and Montana. Their territory stretched almost to the North Saskatchewan River in the north and the Missouri River in the south. Today, they live on the Blood, Piegan, and Blackfoot **Reserves** in Alberta, Canada, and the Blackfeet Reservation in Montana in the United States.

The Blackfoot people live in two worlds today: they honor their heritage while they participate in modern North American society.

10

Like many ancient peoples, the Blackfoot tell their own traditional story about their creation. In the beginning, everything was covered with water. Old Man (Napi) sent the Otter, Beaver, and Muskrat to dive down and get some earth. They failed, but Duck returned with some earth in his foot, which the Old Man took in his hand and dropped. Rain was sent, and everything grew on the earth. Old Man and Old Woman, the only two people in the world, decided how life would be for everyone. Old Man later created everything on the earth, including people, by forming them with some clay and breathing on them (see pages 28–29).

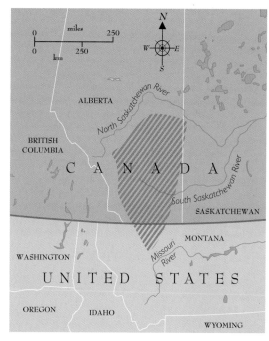

The traditional lands of the Blackfoot people covered the plains east of the Rocky Mountains in both the United States and Canada.

The Blackfoot people's name came from the neighboring Cree people, who called them *siksikauw*, or "black-footed people," because the bottoms of their moccasins were black. The Blackfoot people call themselves *Niitsitapii*, or "the real people."

Blackfoot Language

Nearly six thousand Blackfoot in Canada and the United States speak their native tongue. Here are a few words of their language:

Blackfoot	Pronunciation	English
imitaa	ih-mih-tah	dog
iinnii	ih-nih	buffalo
makoiyi	mah-guh-ih-yih	wolf
natosi	nah-tuh-sih	sun
oki	uh-gih	hello
pis-skaan	bihs-sgahn	buffalo jump

Chapter 2

BEFORE CONTACT

The Blackfoot tribes originally lived in northeastern Canada and Maine and slowly moved southwest to the plains of Saskatchewan, Alberta, and Montana. They used dogs and travois (a simple sled made with two poles holding a platform for a load), following the buffalo as they moved from the open prairie in the summer and fall to the more sheltered forests in the winter.

Constantly at war over territory and access to the buffalo with neighboring tribes, the Blackfoot people were surprised and defeated in 1730 when, for the first time, the Shoshones rode horses into battle. They knew that they also had to have horses

To gather foods and hunt, the Blackfoot people often moved their camps. Tepees and household goods were packed onto a travois, which was originally pulled by a large dog and later a horse.

This painted hide shows a buffalo hunt. For the Blackfoot people, buffalo provided food, hides for tepees, and buffalo robes for wearing and trading.

and turned to their **allies**, probably the Flathead, Kootenai, or Nez Perce Indians, for help in getting them. The Cree Indians gave them another advantage — the rifle, which they had obtained from European traders.

Winter Counts

Before they had a writing system, some of the Blackfoot people kept a record of their tribal history using pictures, sometimes painting them onto **hides** or buffalo robes. Each winter, a certain person in camp remembered one important event for that year — a battle, an **epidemic**, or unusual weather — and told others about it. Later, pictures were drawn onto paper each winter. These documents are called winter counts.

When many Blackfoot bands gathered to camp together in the summer, each band, and each family in the band, had a certain spot where they always put their tepee.

EARLY CONTACT

By 1754, when a Hudson's Bay Company trader first wrote about the Blackfoot people, they were mounted on horses and knew about metal axes, knives, and other items the Europeans brought to exchange with other Native groups. Blackfoot tribes began trading in the 1780s, carrying dried meat, buffalo robes, and furs to British forts. Among the first European Americans the Blackfoot people saw were those from the Meriwether Lewis and William Clark expedition of 1804 to 1806, sent by President Thomas Jefferson.

A TIME OF TRADE

American **trappers** competed with the Blackfoot hunters to sell furs at the trading posts. Thus, the American trappers and traders who came north on the Missouri River after Lewis and Clark were regarded as enemies and driven out of Blackfoot country. The Blackfoot view of the Americans improved when the American Fur Company made peace with the people and built a fort for trading on the upper Missouri River in 1831.

CONFLICTS AND TREATIES

After the discovery of gold in California in 1849, settlers poured west; many conflicts arose between them and the Blackfoot people. In 1855, Isaac Stevens, the governor of the Northwest Territory, which included Blackfoot land, signed a **treaty** with the tribe, which they called the Lame Bull Treaty. The Blackfoot people were promised the sole use of a large area of Montana as a reservation, annual payments in goods, and training to be ranchers and farmers if they would leave the settlers alone

At trading posts, the Blackfoot people exchanged furs for guns.

An Evil Exchange

The era from 1830 to 1850 became known as the "whiskey trade" time, when the Blackfoot people exchanged buffalo robes for whiskey and other trade goods from traders. The whiskey and the diseases brought by the traders, such as smallpox, measles, and tuberculosis, were a disaster for the tribe. It was estimated that from 1868 to 1873, about 25 percent of the tribe died from drinking alcohol and the fighting, killing, and freezing to death that resulted from drunkenness.

Miners like these wanted to look for copper and gold in the Montana mountains and pressured the U.S. government to buy more than 1 million acres (405,000 hectares) from the Blackfoot people and move the native residents out. Nothing of mineral value was found, but the beautiful mountain area later became Glacier National Park.

and allow the railroads and telegraphs to be built on their land. Later treaties, government orders and laws, and agreements with the United States reduced their Montana reservation to a fraction of its original size.

Some Blackfoot people fought the invading settlers and miners during the Blackfoot War of 1865 to 1870. The only U.S. military action against the Blackfoot tribe, the Marias River Massacre, occurred in 1870, when Major Eugene Baker attacked Blackfoot chief Heavy Runner's camp by mistake and killed about two hundred innocent people, including women and children.

In 1870, the Hudson's Bay Company, which owned all of western Canada, sold the Blackfoot territory to the Canadian government. In 1877, the government signed Treaty 7 with the Blackfoot tribes living in Canada. Although they did not understand the treaty, the Blackfoot chiefs agreed to give up 50,000 square miles

(129,500 square kilometers) of hunting grounds in exchange for reserves, annual payments, and tools for farming and ranching. Most of the people continued their traditional hunting lifestyles until the buffalo herds were shot by American hide hunters.

> The white people thought they were coming into empty land. We had a life and a system going here, and it's still ongoing.
>
> *Pat Provost, Northern Piegan, from* The Story of the Blackfoot People, *2001*

RESERVATION LIFE

After the disappearance of the buffalo, around 1879, the Blackfoot people had no choice but to move to their government-assigned lands and try to make a living in a different way. Poorly prepared to make this change, many people died during the Starvation Winter of 1883 to 1884.

In Montana, the Southern Piegans moved onto their reservation and became known as the Blackfeet. Beginning in 1907, the U.S. government forced them to divide the reservation land into individual parcels and opened the rest of their land to

Mountain Chief

Born "Ninastoko" in southern Alberta, Canada, in 1848, Mountain Chief was the last Blackfoot **hereditary** chief. At eighteen years old, he began fighting bravely against the Crow and the Kootenai Indians. He sold the Glacier National Park lands to the U.S. government in 1895. Later in life, he lectured the tourists at Glacier National Park about his tribe and their traditional way of life. He died at age ninety-four.

Established as a national park in 1910, Glacier is home to more than 70 species of mammals and 260 species of birds.

Upon the death of a Blackfoot chief, certain personal belongings were kept with his body, and the rest of his wealth was distributed to the tribe according to his wishes. These people are dividing up the wealth of a chief who died around 1901.

white settlers. This division continued until the Indian Reorganization Act of 1934. The tribe adopted a constitution and formed a council to oversee their reservation lands in 1935.

The Piikani, Kainai, and Siksika all moved onto their Canadian reserves and were pressured to give up their lands as well. Only the Kainai were able to keep their reserve from shrinking; it remains the largest reserve in Canada.

All the tribes became dependent upon government food **rations** and tried to become ranchers and farmers, building log cabins to live in. Christian **missionaries** started boarding schools and took the children away from their homes to educate them, usually forcing them to abandon their Native culture.

DURING AND AFTER THE WAR

During World War II (1939–1945), many men moved off the Blackfeet Reservation and joined the U.S. military, where they learned new skills. The remaining Blackfeet ranched and raised farm animals on their lands. A 1964 flood resulted in emergency money being given to the reservation to build houses, roads, and dams.

After the war, the Canadian government began to improve **social services** on the reserves, where most of the Canadian Blackfoot people remained, and began a strong agricultural program. By the 1970s, modern housing and electricity were introduced to the Canadian Blackfoot reserves.

In the 1950s, alcohol sales were allowed on U.S. Blackfeet land and in the 1960s on Canadian reserves, encouraging **alcoholism** and creating many health and social problems. By the 1960s, many Blackfoot children on both sides of the border attended **integrated** schools and went on to college, returning to the reservation or reserves to work as managers, welfare officers, teachers, and nurses. In 1976, Red Crow College opened on the Blood Reserve and Blackfeet Community College on the Blackfeet Reservation. Much of the reservation and reserve social life revolves around sports such as rodeo, hockey, and basketball.

World War II was the first time that many Blackfeet people left the reservation. Here at Camp Lejeune, North Carolina, Marine Corps reservists Minnie Spotted Wolf (Blackfeet), Celia Mix (Potawatomi), and Viola Eastman (Ojibwe) pose in their uniforms in 1943.

People ask me if we will ever get along. When will Indians and whites have respect for each other? I think the time is coming.

Blackfeet member
Ben Calf Robe

TRADITIONAL WAY OF LIFE

Chapter 3

BLACKFOOT ANNUAL CYCLE

The Blackfoot bands were nomadic, moving often. They spent the longest time in their winter camp, which was in a sheltered river valley, beginning in late October or early November. Each band wintered separately, erecting their tepees in the woods so that the trees helped shield them from the icy winds. They wore buffalo-fur hats, mittens, moccasins, and robes with the fur on the inside to keep warm. The men hunted when they could; when no fresh game was found, the Blackfoot people ate dried meat, roots, and **pemmican**.

When they saw the geese flying north, usually in March, the bands knew that it was time to leave their winter camp. The men hunted small animals until the band caught up with the buffalo, which had moved out of the woods earlier. Spring was the time to gather new tepee poles, make clothing for the warm weather, and repair riding equipment. Women looked for new spring greens and fresh foods.

In June, the bands gathered for the annual tribal buffalo hunt in the same place as in earlier years,

Everyday moccasins worn by the Blackfoot people were plain buffalo hide with the fur inside for warmth. Beautiful beaded moccasins were worn on special occasions.

and each took their same spot in the circle of bands. The hunt provided lots of fresh meat, new buffalo hides for tepees and clothing, and buffalo tongues for the Sun Dance. The Sun Dance ceremony, an annual gathering that was both religious and social, began in August. A time for feasting, wearing fancy clothes, and meeting friends from other bands, it also provided an opportunity for dancing and singing for the good of the tribe.

> What is life?
> It is the flashes
> of a firefly
> in the night.
>
> *Crowfoot (1830–1890),*
> *chief of the Blackfoot*
> *Confederacy*

After the Sun Dance ceremony was over, the bands split up for their fall buffalo-hunting activities. The bands moved as much as necessary to stay with the buffalo so the men could continue hunting, while the women gathered berries and dried the buffalo meat for pemmican. If there was extra food and buffalo robes, the band would visit a trading post to trade for pots, pans, knives, rifles, and other goods. As the weather worsened, the band moved into its winter camp.

Buffalo Jumps

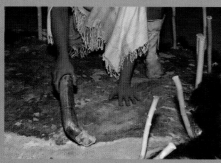

The traditional way to prepare a buffalo hide. After pegging the hide to the ground with the fur side down, a woman scrapes it with a bone tool.

One of the ways that the Blackfoot tribes hunted buffalo was to panic them so that they ran off a cliff. Then the men would kill them and the women would skin them and cut up the meat. The cliffs used for this were called "buffalo jumps." One of the most famous is Head-Smashed-In Buffalo Jump in Alberta, Canada, which Native Americans used for over six thousand years. Over one hundred such buffalo jumps have been found in North America.

Born in 1872, John Two Guns was adopted at an early age by Blackfeet chief White Calf and became chief himself upon White Calf's death in 1902. He was often photographed with tourists at Glacier National Park until his death in 1934.

SOCIAL ORGANIZATION

The Blackfoot bands were small, extended family groups with no formal organization other than a recognized leader. If a band became too large, the people would split into two smaller bands. Bands used names based upon some event or the people in them, such as Many Fat Horses band and All Short People band.

Leaders were men who were brave warriors and generous to the poor. They worked hard to keep order, ending arguments and making final decisions for all of the people.

Men hunted animals for food, cared for their horses, and protected their band and its territory. They were away from camp a lot, hunting and leading raids, while women's lives were based in camp. Women prepared food, raised children, and cared for the sacred bundles, which were a group of objects tied in a cloth or hide package that they used for religious ceremonies. Because the women owned the tepees and everything inside them, they were responsible for preparing dried foods such as pemmican, **tanning** hides, and sewing and decorating clothes and tepees.

Warrior Societies

Made from a buffalo's thick neck hide, war shields were usually about 3 feet (1 meter) in diameter. Sacred or protective symbols covered each shield.

Grouped by age, each traditional warrior society had special clothing, songs, and dances. These societies assisted the band's leader by organizing hunts, warfare, and camp moves. The societies with the best warriors had the highest status. Often using horses or weapons, young men had to buy a membership in a lower society, usually from someone who was about to buy his way into a higher society. The Piegan had the following warrior societies, beginning with the youngest: Pigeons, Mosquitoes, Braves, All Brave Dogs, Front Tails, Raven Bearers, Dogs, Kit Foxes, Catchers, and Buffalo Bulls. Together, the groups were known as the "All Comrades" societies.

CHILDHOOD

When a child was about to be born, the mother left camp and was cared for by a **medicine woman**. After birth, the baby was washed, prayed over, and painted red. The baby's **umbilical cord** was cut with an arrowhead and then dried and preserved in a beaded container: a snake shape for a boy's and a lizard shape for a girl's. Blackfoot people believed that snakes and lizards were never sick and lived long lives, and they wished this for their children. A few days after birth, the father asked a relative or important person to officially name the baby. This name was a girl's forever, but a boy could earn many names throughout his life based upon what he did.

Boys and girls played together until they were about five years old, then mothers began to teach the girls their responsibilities. The girls started by gathering wood, picking berries, and digging roots. They helped their mothers, soon learning how to prepare food, tan hides, and put up and take down a tepee. Fathers trained their sons to shoot with bows and arrows, guard horses, and follow animal tracks. When a boy killed his first animal or a girl finished her first beadwork, the family held a feast to celebrate.

This beaded buckskin shirt was made by a Blackfoot woman for her husband or son to wear on special occasions.

Headdress

Worn by war leaders and **elders**, the traditional Blackfoot headdress was a crown of eagle feathers standing straight up on the head. The feathers sometimes had horsehair attached; white weasel tails hung down from the band. Each eagle feather in the headdress was the symbol of a story about the person who wore it. These headdresses were sacred and protected the wearer during battle.

This Kainai (Blood) chief wears the traditional Blackfoot warrior's headdress with standing eagle feathers resembling a crown.

ADULT LIFE

Between the ages of fifteen and twenty, a young man might go on a **vision quest** with the help of a medicine man. Men usually married after age twenty-one and could have as many wives as they could afford. Parents arranged marriages, and the families exchanged gifts, usually horses.

After death, important men were sewn into their tepees with their possessions, and their horses were killed to provide them with transportation to the land of the dead. Other men and women had their possessions wrapped with their bodies, and their bodies were placed in trees or other high places so animals wouldn't scatter their bones.

According to Blackfoot custom, a dead body is wrapped in hides and placed in a high place with important personal possessions, such as a war shield. Here, a scaffold built between tree trunks keeps the body off the ground.

This 1920 painting by Joseph Henry Sharp called *Making Sweetgrass Medicine* shows two items that were part of most Blackfoot ceremonial bundles — feathers and sweetgrass, a grass used for spiritual purposes.

RELIGION AND BELIEFS

The most important Blackfoot god was Sun; his wife was Moon, and Morning Star was their child. Many animals and birds also possessed **supernatural** powers, as well as forces of nature such as thunder. Old Man, or Napi, was not only the creator of the world but a **trickster**. There are many Old Man stories where he sometimes behaves foolishly; these stories are told to teach children the correct way to act in life.

Most ceremonies were based on medicine bundles, which were sacred. Each one was different. Usually, a young man would go away from the camp and stay out for several nights. He **fasted** and called upon the gods and spirits to give him power. They would come to him in a dream, give him a power, and show him the items that should be in his sacred medicine bundle. Then it was up to him to gather the objects for his medicine bundle. Sometimes the man would also be shown designs to paint on his tepee.

Sacred or Medicine Bundles

For the Blackfoot peoples, sacred bundles held the symbols of supernatural power. Painted tepees, standup headdresses, and other special items were also thought of as medicine bundles, or sacred bundles. Most bundles contained items needed to perform a ceremony, such as tobacco, paint, and sweetgrass. A bundle might also contain a pipe, a war shirt, tepee flag, knife, lance, or shield, all wrapped in skins or cloth and treated in certain ways to protect their power. Medicine bundles could be bought from another person.

The Blackfoot people adopted the Sun Dance from other Plains tribes, probably in the early 1800s. Their most important ceremony, it was called the Medicine Lodge. A respected woman always planned and paid for this ceremony. She made a promise to the gods and organized the ceremony to fulfill her promise. This involved buying the medicine bundle from the previous sponsor of the Medicine Lodge, supplying hundreds of buffalo tongues, and building a lodge using one hundred willows.

This Blackfoot warrior is participating in the Sun Dance by tying himself to a center pole with strips of leather that are pierced through his skin. He will dance until his skin tears and he pulls free, showing his bravery and dedication to his community.

How Old Man Created the World

The Blackfoot have a **myth** to explain how Old Man, or Napi, created the Earth and everything on it. At first, there was no land, only a great ocean. Old Man took mud from the bottom of the ocean, rolled it in his hands, and threw it onto the water, where it grew into land.

Then, Old Man walked across the land, creating mountains, rivers, and all the other features we know today. At the same time, he also created the animals and plants to live on the land.

Sometimes, Old Man made mistakes. At first, he placed bighorn sheep on the prairies and antelopes on the mountains. But bighorn sheep are animals that climb steep, rocky slopes with ease, and antelopes prefer to run at great speed across the prairies. When Old Man saw that the animals were unhappy he moved the bighorn sheep to the mountains and the antelopes to the prairies.

Before 1800, there were millions of bighorn sheep in North America, so it is not surprising that they are featured in Blackfoot myths. Over many centuries, the Blackfoot people would have observed their behavior and admired their climbing skills.

Young Blackfoot women collecting goldenrod around 1910. Goldenrod is one of the medicinal plants used frequently by Native Americans. This is one of the plants that Old Man would have shown to the Blackfoot people.

Finally, Old Man decided to create people. He formed them out of clay, but they knew nothing and were helpless. Old Man had to teach them how to survive. He led them through the prairies, swamps, and forests, explaining which plants were good to eat and which were cures for sickness. He also showed them how to make bows and arrows out of wood, feathers, and sharp stones, so that they could kill animals to eat. And since these animals had to be cooked, Old Man explained how to make fire.

The people also needed to know about spirit power. Old Man told them to sleep and dream. He said that an animal would come to each of them in a dream and advise them. They must obey the animal and later, when they needed help and prayed to their animal, it would hear them and come to their aid.

BLACKFOOT LIFE TODAY

Chapter 4

CONTEMPORARY BLACKFOOT PEOPLE

Educational and employment opportunities continue to improve for the Blackfoot people, but they are still dealing with the social problems created by allowing businesses to serve alcohol on the reserves and reservations in the 1950s and 1960s. Currently, all the reserves and reservations have social services for alcoholism, **addiction**, family problems, and unemployment.

The Canadian reserves have focused on tribal independence. These tribes have slowly taken control of the health, social, economic, and educational services on their reserves so that they can include tribal language and traditions in the schools and other services.

The Kainai (Blood) reserve is the largest in Canada and supports a farming operation, growing grain and other crops. The Piikani (Piegan) reserve owns a successful clothing factory and sells arts and crafts to visitors. The elders help at Head-Smashed-In National Monument, explaining their traditional way of life to the tourists. The Siksika (Northern Blackfoot) reserve, containing 175,400 acres (71,000 ha) of land, is still in the final stages of arranging self-government with Canada.

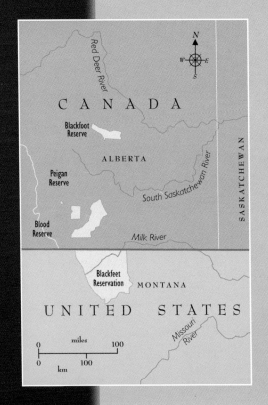

Today, the people of the Blackfoot Confederation live on three reserves in Canada and one reservation in the United States. The Siksika (Northern Blackfoot), Piikani (Piegan), and Kainai (Blood) people each have a reserve in Canada, while the southern Piegan occupy the Blackfeet Reservation in Montana.

30

Intertribal powwows, hosted by the Blackfoot people and other Indian nations, give everyone the opportunity to celebrate their traditional heritage and teach others about it. Here, a young boy performs at a Blackfeet Reservation powwow.

In the United States, the Blackfeet Reservation, on 1.5 million acres (607,300 ha) in northwest Montana, relies on tourism dollars, as the reservation is located next to the popular Glacier National Park. The reservation has also opened a **casino** and it **leases** tribal land to oil and natural gas companies. Another source of income is farming, mainly of beef cattle.

All of the Blackfoot nations have an elected council of leaders that makes decisions for the tribe. The three Canadian tribes belong to an organization of Treaty 7 tribes as well as the national First Nations Council.

Native Americans of many tribes have adopted rodeo as a favorite sport and participate in regular rodeo events and championships. The Blackfoot tribes, however, organized their own Indian Rodeo Cowboy Association in 1962. All of the Blackfoot tribes also host **powwows** on their lands each year.

A Unique Culture Continues

All of the Blackfoot tribes are concerned with maintaining their unique language and culture while improving and increasing the jobs available on their reserves. By taking control of the schools that their children attend, they feel they can again take part in their education and share the traditional Blackfoot values. The Blackfoot language is taught in preschool, elementary school, and high school programs on the reserves. The Red Crow College in Alberta, Canada, with a new Kainai Studies degree program, and the Blackfeet Community College in Montana are both tribal colleges.

[The hotshots are] like the Marines of the firefighters. We're the first ones that go over there and the last ones to leave, mostly. So you see a lot of action, and it's scary, but you get used to it.

Nicole Meeso, Chief Mountain Hotshot, 2003

Because of increased opportunities on the reservation and reserves, these Blackfeet girls growing up today have an opportunity to learn the Blackfoot language and go to college.

Chief Mountain Hotshots

The only Native American firefighting crew in their region that is sent to the most dangerous fires, the Chief Mountain Hotshots may work on fifteen to twenty large fires in the United States and Canada each year. A small group of highly trained and well-respected firefighters, they have had a movie made about their lives called *Fire Warriors*. This group of men and women feel that their warrior heritage helps them to be "the best of the best."

Teachers at the immersion school in Browning, Montana, speak and write only in the Blackfoot language to help the young children in their classes become fluent in their traditional language.

On the Blackfeet reservation, the Piegan Institute has promoted the Blackfoot language since 1987. It runs an immersion school in Browning, Montana, where children from kindergarten to grade 8 are taught in their native language, and no English is spoken. The Piegan Institute also produces written, audio, and video information on Blackfoot language and history.

BLACKFOOT LITERATURE

Beverly Hungry Wolf has written several books about the Blackfoot people, including two which focus on Blackfoot women. *The Ways of My Grandmothers* (1980) features stories about women collected from respected older Blackfoot women in Canada. *Daughters of the Buffalo Women: Maintaining the Tribal Faith* (1996) is a collection of memories of older women who grew up in the early 1900s on reservations and in boarding schools.

> By tribal custom, all the old women of the past are my grandmothers.
> *Beverly Hungry Wolf*

James Welch, Blackfeet author, described life on the reservation in some of his world-famous novels, such as *The Death of Jim Loney*. He died in 2003.

Probably the person best known in the Blackfoot arts and literature world is author James Welch (1940–2003). Winner of the American Book Award, the Native Writers' Circle's Lifetime Achievement Award in 1997, and many other awards, Welch is best known for portraying Native American life when it conflicts with modern white society. Welch also wrote poetry and one nonfiction book about Custer and the Battle of Little Bighorn, told from a Native American point of view.

> Although I consider myself a storyteller first and foremost, I hope my books will help educate people who don't understand how or why Indian people often feel lost in America.
>
> *Author James Welch, 2001*

Harold Gray (Long Standing Bear Chief), who died in 2010, also wrote about the Native American way of life, producing many books and articles for both adults and children.

Returning Tribal Treasures

In 2000, the Glenbow Museum in Calgary, Canada, returned 251 sacred objects, including medicine pipes, headdresses, and medicine bundles that they had in their collections, to the Blackfoot Confederacy. Some had been purchased from **descendants** of the traders; Native Americans, fearing the items would be lost, gave others to the museum long ago. Now these articles have been returned, and the confederacy has joined with the museum to create their own display and publish a book.

Because of a new law, museums are returning many traditional and sacred objects, such as this ceremonial knife and sheath, to the Blackfoot Confederacy.

BLACKFOOT ART AND ARCHITECTURE

Gale Running Wolf Sr. is a Blackfoot artist working in pencil and acrylic paints. Using blue and white paints, he portrays his heritage in a special style and has won over thirty-five awards for his art. His pictures are in shows, galleries, and museums all over the United States. Many other Blackfoot artists, musicians, and writers add to the arts scene in both Canada and the United States.

The architect Douglas Cardinal was born in Alberta, Canada, in 1934, of Blackfoot descent. His curved style of building can be seen in the Canadian Museum of Civilization in Gatineau, Quebec, and in the First Nations University of Canada in Regina, Saskatchewan.

Douglas Cardinal was responsible for the overall design of the Smithsonian National Museum of the American Indian in Washington, D.C.

Blackfoot Moccasins and Beadwork

The Blackfoot people have always been known for their moccasins. Left plain for daily wear, moccasins were decorated with fancy beading for special occasions. Because Blackfoot women used stiff porcupine quills to decorate moccasins, early designs were **geometrical**. When beads became available at trading posts, they began to design curved patterns. Using solid white or blue beads for the background, Blackfoot women created new flower designs as well as following traditional patterns. Today's Blackfoot artists sometimes bead moccasins using the very old traditional designs, but they often borrow designs from other Native American tribes or use the popular Blackfoot flower designs in their beadwork.

Top: Colorful beadwork decorates this traditional Blackfoot hide dress, worn at a contemporary powwow.

Bottom: Jackie Larson Bread is a well-known Blackfoot beadwork artist in Montana. As a child she watched her grandmother bead and later she studied historic beadwork at the Museum of the Plains Indian in Browning, Montana. She specializes in portraits, flowers, and geometrical designs.

Chapter 5

CURRENT BLACKFOOT ISSUES

WORKING TOGETHER

In 1998, all four of the Blackfoot tribes began a movement to reestablish the Blackfoot Confederacy, made up of the Siksika, Piikani, and Kainai tribes from Canada and the U.S. Blackfeet. The Blackfoot Confederacy represents all the Blackfoot people and can work with museums to bring home tribal treasures, address border difficulties between countries, and bring jobs and government funding to the tribes.

Blackfeet people from Montana form part of the honor guard at the 2010 Memorial Day Ceremony at Arlington National Cemetery, Virginia.

Feathers across the Border

Since the Blackfoot Confederacy has tribes on both sides of the U.S.– Canadian border, there can sometimes be problems when members try to get together. In June 2002, Canadian Kainai Chief Chris Shade couldn't bring his eagle-feather headdress across the border into the United States. In the United States, Native Americans are allowed to have eagle feathers for religious purposes, but they must have a permit since eagles are a protected species by law. Because Canada doesn't have the same law, Chief Shade had no permit, and his headdress had to stay home in Canada.

A BRIGHT FUTURE

In 2009, the Blackfeet Tribal Business Council created a new company called Chief Mountain Technologies, based in Browning, Montana. It should create many jobs for tribal members in the fields of computing and business services for government organizations. Tribal members are also now benefiting from money paid to the nation by oil companies that are looking for new sources of oil.

The Blackfoot people are moving forward, solving their own problems, and maintaining the important traditions that make them who they are.

Today, they're trying to separate us. But that borderline is nothing. It's invisible to us.

Earl Old Person, chief of the Blackfeet tribe, referring to the U.S.-Canadian border in 2002

A member of the Albertan group Blackfoot Medicine Speaks rests after dancing at the Smithsonian Folklife Festival in Washington, D.C.

TIMELINE

1690	Hudson's Bay Trading Company makes contact with Blackfoot people in Alberta.
1730	Shoshones on horseback fight Blackfoot tribes on foot.
1730–1750	Blackfoot tribes acquire horses; first European missionaries and fur trappers arrive.
about 1780	Blackfoot tribes trade for guns.
1780–1805	Shoshones suffer horrible defeats by the Blackfoot warriors.
1787	Northwest Fur Company begins trading with Siksika and Kainai tribes.
1803	United States buys most of Montana from France.
1819	Measles kills one-third of Blackfoot people.
1824	Beginning of war with fur trappers.
1833	Karl Bodmer paints portraits of Blackfoot leaders.
1830s–1860s	Smallpox and scarlet fever kill around 10,000 Blackfoot people.
1849	Discovery of gold in California brings many people through Blackfoot territory.
1855	Lame Bull's Treaty is signed, the first one between the United States and a Blackfoot tribe.
1860	White settlers begin to enter Blackfoot territory.
1865–1870	American settlers and Indians collide in Blackfoot War.
1870	Marias River Massacre; Canada owns most Blackfoot land.
1873	Blackfeet Reservation is established in Montana.
1877	Canada and three Blackfoot tribes sign Treaty 7, further reducing the tribes' lands; Piegan, Siksika (Blackfoot), and Blood (Kainai) reservations are created.
1882	Blood people move to a new reservation in Canada.
1883–84	Since white hunters have killed off the buffalo on which the Blackfoot depend, many die during Starvation Winter.

1885	U.S. government takes away part of the Blackfoot Reservation for mineral exploitation.
1893	Great Northern Transcontinental Railroad is finished through Blackfoot territory, bringing more people to Blackfoot lands.
1892	First boarding school for Blackfeet children opens.
1894	Town of Browning is established on Blackfeet Reservation.
1895	Blackfeet sell land to United States for $1.5 million; it becomes Glacier National Park.
1903	Fence built around Blackfeet Reservation; first Blackfeet Tribal Council elected.
1907	U.S. government forces the Blackfeet to divide their reservation land between individual tribal members.
1934	The U.S. Indian Reorganization Act aids in the modern economic and political development of the Blackfeet tribe.
1939–45	World War II: many Blackfoot men enlist in the military.
1941	Museum of the Plains Indian is established in Browning, Montana.
1962	Blackfoot people organize the Indian Rodeo Cowboy Association.
1976	Blackfeet Community College and Red Crow College open.
1986	Piegan Institute is created.
1988	Chief Mountain Hotshots firefighting crew is formed.
1998	Blackfoot Confederacy is reestablished.
2000	Glenbow Museum in Calgary, Canada, returns 251 objects to the Blackfoot Confederacy.
2003	James Welch, Blackfeet author, dies.
2009	Blackfeet Tribal Business Council sets up Chief Mountain Technologies to create jobs in computing and business services.

GLOSSARY

addiction: being unable to resist consuming a specific substance or taking part in an activity.

alcoholism: an addiction to alcohol.

allies: groups with friendly political relationships.

ancestors: people from whom an individual or group is descended.

boarding schools: places where students must live at the school.

casino: a building that has slot machines and other gambling games.

confederation: groups of people or nations joined for a common purpose.

constitution: the basic laws and principles of a nation that outline the powers of the government and the rights of the people.

culture: the arts, beliefs, and customs that make up a people's way of life.

descendants: people descended from a particular person.

discrimination: unjust treatment, usually because of a person's race or sex.

elder: a tribal leader.

environment: objects and conditions all around that affect living things and communities.

epidemic: a sudden increase of a rapidly spreading disease.

fasted: went without eating.

floodplain: the area of land beside a river or stream that is covered with water during a flood.

geometrical: describes a design with regular lines and shapes.

hereditary: describes something that can be passed on to one's children or gained from one's parents.

hides: the skins of animals.

ice age: a period of time when the earth is very cold and lots of water in the oceans turns to ice.

integrated: open to people of all races.

irrigation: any system for watering the land to grow plants.

lease: allow someone to use land or property for a specified time in return for money.

medicine woman or man: a healer and spiritual leader.

migration: movement from one place to another.

missionaries: people who try to teach others their religion.

myth: a traditional story that explains beliefs or events in nature.

nomadic: not having a single home but moving from place to place in search of food or following groups of animals.

pemmican: dried meat, pounded into a powder and mixed with fat and dried berries.

persecution: treating someone or a certain group of people badly over a period of time.

powwows: celebrations of Indian culture often marking specific events; usually include singing, drumming, dancing, and giving thanks.

prejudice: dislike or injustice that is not based on reason or experience.

rations: food allowances given out a little at a time.

reservation: land set aside by the U.S. government for specific Native American tribes to live on.

reserves: land set aside by the Canadian government for First Nations (Native American) tribes.

social services: services provided by the government or other organizations to help the needy, poor, or sick.

supernatural: beyond the natural world; something that cannot be seen, especially relating to gods and spirits.

tanning: changing animal skin into leather by soaking it in a liquid containing acid.

trapper: a person who catches wild animals for their fur.

treaty: an agreement among two or more nations.

trickster: a character in different stories who is both foolish and wise.

umbilical cord: a flexible structure that connects the baby to the mother in the womb.

vision quest: a journey to seek spiritual power from the supernatural world.

MORE RESOURCES

WEBSITES:

http://www.bloodtribe.org
The Blood tribe's website includes a virtual tour of the reservation and a brief history of the tribe.

http://www.blackfeetnation.com
The Blackfeet Nation's website contains a history, timeline, creation story, and other information about the tribe.

http://www.angelfire.com/ar/waakomimm/midi.html
Contains sound files of Blackfoot music.

http://www.angelfire.com/ar/waakomimm/peigan.html
Click on this Northern Piikani and Southern Piegan website to read stories about Head-Smashed-In Buffalo Jump, see pictures of leaders, or listen to Blackfoot music, including kids' powwow songs.

http://www.angelfire.com/ar/waakomimm/sikblf.html
For the history, art, and music of the Siksika. Scroll down the website to find various stories.

http://www.bigorrin.org/blackfoot_kids.htm
Online Blackfoot Indian fact sheet for kids.

http://www.head-smashed-in.com/
The website of the Head-Smashed-In Buffalo Jump UNESCO World Heritage Site in Alberta.

http://www.legendsofamerica.com/na-blackfootlegends.html
Blackfoot legends and historic photographs.

http://www.native-languages.org/blackfoot.htm
Site about the Blackfoot language, including vocabulary, grammar, pronunciation, and writing system.

http://www.native-languages.org/blackfoot-legends.htm
Blackfoot legends and traditional stories.

http://www.trailtribes.org/greatfalls/home.htm
The Blackfeet section of trailtribes.org looks at traditional and contemporary Blackfeet culture and the tribe's relationship with the United States.

BOOKS:

Ditchfield, Christin. *The Blackfoot (True Books)*. Children's Press, 2006.

Gibson, Karen Bush. *The Blackfeet: People of the Dark Moccasins (American Indian Nations)*. Bridgestone Books, 2003.

Gibson, Karen Bush. *Native American History for Kids: With 21 Activities*. Chicago Review Press, 2010.

Hungry Wolf, Beverly. *The Ways of My Grandmothers*. Harper Paperbacks, 1998.

King, David C. *First People*. DK Children, 2008.

King, David C. *The Blackfeet (First Americans)*. Benchmark Books, 2009.

Murdoch, David S. *North American Indian (DK Eyewitness Books)*. DK Children, 2005.

Patent, Dorothy Hinshaw. *The Buffalo and the Indians: A Shared Destiny*. Clarion Books, 2006.

Press, Petra. *The Blackfeet (First Reports/Native Americans)*. Compass Point Books, 2001.

Rebus, Anna. *Blackfoot (Aboriginal Peoples)*. Weigl Publishers, 2010.

Rebus, Anna. *Head-Smashed-In Buffalo Jump (Wonders of Canada)*. Weigl Publishers, 2007.

THINGS TO THINK ABOUT AND DO

WINTER COUNT

Using paper and colored pencils or paints, draw a winter count for your family, school, community, or church group. What was one important event that happened each year for the last three years? You should have three pictures showing those important events.

NAME THAT BAND

Blackfoot bands were often named for an event that they participated in or for something about the people in them, such as the Never Laughs Band and Gopher Eaters Band. If your class were a band, what would it be named? Why? Draw pictures of the special face painting your band might use or of a flag they might carry.

BORDER DEBATE

Chief Chris Shade wants to bring his traditional headdress from Canada to a Blackfoot Confederacy gathering in the United States. Since he has no permit for the eagle feathers in his headdress, U.S. Customs, a government agency, will take his headdress when he crosses the border. Form a group to discuss the problems his action raises. What do you think should be done?

INDEX